Volker von Schintling-Horny

AF214886

The Been in Sevenstar

Volker von Schintling-Horny

 # The Been

in Sevenstar

A "Sevenstar" expells the Varroa and harmonizes
the Earth in the bees' collecting zone.

Ratingen 2019

Saviour, take the bees in custody,
Which serve the Altar with wax,
Which nourish us with honey,
Which teach us diligence and order,
Which maintain God's creation for us,
Which grant us insight in His reign.
God's blessing may be with them –
Saviour, take the bees in custody.

Volker von Schintling-Horny

 # The Been

in Sevenstar

A "Sevenstar" expells the Varroa and harmonizes
the Earth in the bees' collecting zone.

Verlag und Druck: tredition GmbH, Halenreie 40-44, 22359 Hamburg, Germany www.tredition.de
Author: Volker von Schintling-Horny
schintling@schintlinghorny.de
www.schintlinghorny.de   Tel. +49 2102 31110
Translator: Raffael Grüner
Lektorat: Alexandra Eryiğit-Klos
ISBN 978-3-7482-8958-6 (Paperback)
      978-3-7482-8959-3 (Hardcover)
      978-3-7482-8960-9 (e-book)

10th edition, March 2019

Printout with specification of source is **desired**.
Volker von Schintling-Horny 2019

Content

PREFACE

In 1991, the first booklet of Heinrich Sannemann's "Gelbe Reihe" (yellow series) was published by UKKAM Publishers under the title *Der Bien und seine wahre Aufgabe auf Erden* (The Been and its true task on Earth). The booklet has been out of print for a while. But since the booklet has repeatedly been asked for and Mother Earth is continuously being misused and, additionally, the Varroa has become a real problem for many beekeepers, I pick up the ideas of Heinrich Sannemann and pass them on to all beekeepers, summarized and extended by my Sevenstar (heptagram) method, with kind permission of Heinrich Sannemann. Thus, our favourites, the bees, will be relieved from the nasty mites and the Earth will vibrate harmonically inside the area of activity of the Bee-Sevenstar. An often assessed fact is: **"Our bees carry out up to 75% of all pollinations of flowers."** Otherwise we would hardly have any apples, cherries or other fruits in our gardens. The heptagram style is **not** oriented on profit but on **consolidation** of the Been and, with that, on **harmonization of the environment**.

Ratingen, 24th June, 2003

INTRODUCTION

Bees are a very special species of animals because they have been living on Earth in communities with precisely organized tasks of work for 50 million years at least. Such a community is only viable if its limbs - the queen, the female worker bees, the male drones, the honeycomb and the beehouse (hives or skeps) - effectively work together as a whole.

The beefather or -mother (beekeeper) is also an important part of this community because they live in harmony with the colonies and help them by their love and care to survive in today's environment. We refer to such a community as **the Been**.

The Been already lived with the ancient Egyptians, indeed even in earlier times, in state-forming, co-working community, together with humans. Therefore, many characteristics, like the hierarchical order (queen = head of state; brood care = kindergarten; worker = nectar-/pollen collector; guard = soldier; honey = stock keeping; round dance = information systems; matriarchy; comb building = house building), are as inherent in humans as they are in the Been. Is it not autosuggestive that the Been is a very highly developed being on our Earth, comparable to man? The queen has many characteristics of a mother or family father. An active Sevenstar (heptagram) protects itself—and the other economically used colonies that are not standing on the star's tips but produce the necessary honey—in its effective circle like an embankment or a city wall.

In past times, a close connection between human and Been still existed; back then, the "beefather" informed the Been about all important incidents on the farm. The Been can understand our words and our thoughts, but we have forgotten to understand it and can only feel its thoughts mentally. Despite that, the beefather is a very important spiritual part of the entire Been.

The queen bee is the "heart" of the colony: Just as the human cannot live without a heart, the Been cannot live without a queen. There is something special about her, the heart of the colony, because the queen can be a strong individual only if she comes from a swarm cell, i.e., if she grew naturally from the very beginning.
Bringing pollen, nectar, propolis and water are the most important gathering jobs of the worker bees. A colony needs honey from approximately 400 types of flowers for raising their brood. The more types are available, the better.

Instead of lowering the body temperature to go in torpor, as most insects do, a colony of bees resists the cold by with-drawing into a winter cluster and keeping up a temperature of 35–40°C inside and minimum of 10°C outside. The bees create this temperature by contracting the muscles in the wings without moving the wings themselves. They create an energy equal to 40 watt in winter. This energy is enough for outside temperatures down to −30°C and below, but the price for that is approximately 1kg of honey per week.
For comb building, the bees use the wax that is secreted on the underside of the abdomen of the workers after the collection of nectar. To produce 1 gram of wax, the energy of 6 grams of honey is spent. A natural hive inside a hollow tree

is made up of about 100,000 cells in 6 combs, having a surface of about 2.5 square metres. For that, 1.2kg of wax needs to be produced. A natural tree hollow is of a size containing about 25 litres and optimally has its entrance close to the bottom with a diameter of 4cm. The bees will build the combs from top to bottom. The share of the slightly bigger drone combs is about 15% of all combs on average.

About 150,000 bees per day leave the hive and only 148,000 will return, making a loss of 2,000 bees per day. In a warm summer night, a colony will spend more than a liter of water for cooling the combs containing the brood. Therefore, the beekeeper should always install proper watering places close to the hives.

Bees that do not have a job at the moment will be animated by returning collectors to bring nectar by using a special "shaking dance" (Karl von Frisch, 1965). During this dance, the collector will shake its entire body up and down for one or two seconds with about 16 vibrations per second (Hz) while holding the jobless bee with its legs.

For information on new food sources (nectar) in a radius of 50 metres, a round dance is used by the returning bee. With this round dance, only the direction of the location discovered is passed on by showing an angle between the present position of the sun and the direction of the round dance. With the waggle dance, the bee can additionally pass on information about the distance of a discovered location to all interested fellow bees in the hive via the frequency of the dance; for example, five vibrations per quarter minute mean 250 metres of distance. When the fully loaded bees return home from collecting nectar and do not find enough young workers to receive it at the entrance, they will use tools like shaking dances, vibration, circling and forward movement to animate jobless bees as nectar receivers.

Nowadays it is common to increase the number of queen bees (by breeding), which already hints at the fact that they do not grow up naturally. The breeder moves one-day larvae from their worker cell into an artificial bowl that the breeder made of wax—sometimes even a plastic bowl—with a so-called grafting tool. This bowl with the larva is then transferred to a caring colony in which it remains until shortly before the larva hatches. In large-scale productions of queen bees the bowl is even taken out of the caring colonies immediately after capping and then put into a breeding cupboard for further development. This process proves to be unnatural. Colonies with queens bred in such manner do not have an individual character. And the fact that colonies with artificially inseminated queens do not have an individual character goes without saying, from this perspective. Such colonies will slowly degenerate and become unable to defend themselves against diseases. That is why our beloved bees need a protective wall, a town wall with seven watchtowers. Those towers, the tips of the Sevenstar (heptagram), will each be occupied by one swarm colony as "men on guard". In this context, a Sevenstar (heptagram) means the setup of seven colonies in a circle. The vibration energy on a star tip increases so strongly that Varroa mites can hardly dwell among the bees living there. But, of course, even the best Sevenstar would be useless without a bee pasture of sufficient size—otherwise, our beloved bees would just starve to death. Most important for the bees' health is a versatile diet. For proper supply, they need many different types of flowers, for example sunflowers, marigold, borage, centaurea, malva or wild flowers like phacelia, centaurea cyanus, poppy, dandelion, and many more. Healthy, strong bees, strenghtened by a chemical-free tree blossom and a proper bee pasture of 200–600 different species of flowers will survive more easily than those without. Trees like tilia, robinia, willow (for pollen) or mass pastures like rapeseed or mustard seed serve the bees as sources of nectar. The fruit tree blossoms like cherry, apple and plum are a very special source of pasture from which the bees produce honey on a large scale. Also, the comb hygiene should not be neglected. All combs of a hive should be renewed every two years. Due to the loads of incrustations (like the hymens of the bee brood), the combs will turn dark and unhygienic. That makes them an ideal substrate for pathogens - therefore they have to be exchanged regularly. Further information is found in the book *Einfach Imkern* by Dr. Gerhard Liebig (not yet available in English).

3

The copulation of the queen

The Been can only renew itself via division, that is, via swarm formation. But since the natural swarm formation is artificially anticipated by the modern beekeeper—with methods like moving the old hive and offering the returning bees a new hive with feeding- and breeding-combs, or the method of artificial swarming—a natural, strong regeneration of the bees becomes impossible.

A queen originating from a swarm cell flies towards the sun, the gathering site of drones, in its nuptial flight, because she is a sunny animal. The drones as earthy animals have a difficult job getting up there. Only the strongest drones will make it. Here, natural selection is in charge.

The swarm's queen is flying up to the "rainbow height", meaning the height that a rainbow would reach if the weather conditions for it were present. In our latitudes, a rainbow about noon time, when the nuptial flight occurs, reaches a height of approximately 2.1 kilometres. At the equator, the height reaches approximately 3.3 kilometres; towards the poles it decreases. Thus, in that particular height, or more precisely, in the violet zone of the rainbow, the queen will be copulated by about 12 drones.

As the inseminated queen returns to her colony, the spirit of the hive moves in together with her. The bees become "sacred bees". An interesting fact is that bred queens are unable to reach the rainbow height, even if they are allowed to try. They are copulated far below this height.

4

Sevenstar-Rainbow—Cathedral building

Whoever wants to properly grasp the following thought has to imagine the effective area of a Sevenstar as a ball with a diameter of 4.2 kilometres and imagine oneself in the centre of this ball, on the central stone of the Sevenstar.

If bee colonies are brought in relation to such a rainbow dome, what will happen? A comparison with cathedral building will help to understand:

The master architects of early medieval cathedrals constructed their buildings not due to static calculations but due to the laws of harmony and musical chords. The only construction tool they used was a rope with 12 knots. With such a rope, the master architects were able to lay out geometrical figures from which they could "grow" peculiarly vivid beings, like the cathedral of Chartre near Paris.

With this rope one can also lay out an isosceles triangle with side length relations of 5:4:4, in which the two identical angles have 51°25' each. This triangle has its form and angles in common with the Cheops pyramid that continues to be a secret for us in many ways. The same angle is also found in our Sevenstar: 51°25'42".

The Sevenstar with its characteristic angle gave form and rhythm to the early medieval cathedral. Based on the form of the Sevenstar, the entire cathedral is built. In the centre of this Sevenstar lies the holy of holies!

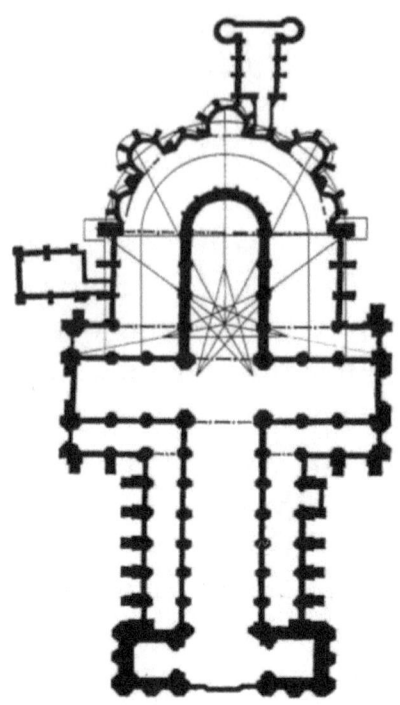

Source: Luis Charpentier p. 125

Abbot Suger wrote about this topic in 1157:

„In the Gothic art of building, the walls become more lightful and lighter in weight, separating walls are missing and the forces and energies playing inside it are divided by pressure and thrust; the pressure curves of the domes are captured by thin vertical pillars and guided widely above the choir corridor and the side nave by the system of vertical pillars. From the 12th century on, the wreath (Sevenstar) of vertical pillars, radiating bravely to all directions, dominates in the impression of Gothic cathedrals. In the ground plan of many Gothic cathedrals in France, the 'Sevenstar' is setting the tone." (Louis Charpentier, The secrets of the Chartre cathedral)

The ground plan of the cathedral clearly shows the intention of the architect to let the Sevenstar in the centre have its effect.

The carry-over to our bees:

Since the Been also is connecting upper and lower worlds, as we just observed about the cathedrals—between sunny aspects of the queen and earthy aspects of the drone—the insights of the cathedral building may be transferred onto the Been.

The cathedral building teaches us that strong vibration energies emit from the Sevenstar, especially from its tips, as long as the angle of 51°25' is kept. So, let's try to use these vibration energies with the Been as amplifier: that very Been that Rudolf Steiner called "much superior to man, for it has already developed further".

Let's guide the blessing of those vibration energies primarily into the Been and, via the Been, also into Mother Earth and ourselves.

5

Templars, origin of the Sevenstar

How come the Templars knew of the Sevenstar? The following explanation is given in the book *Machtwechsel auf der Erde* (Change of power on Earth) by Armin Risi:

"The Templars brought back the Sevenstar knowledge from Jerusalem. After the crusades, the French knights Count Hugues and his nephew travelled to Jerusalem and returned with valuable ideas after a short while. What reason did they have to take that difficult pilgrimage onto themselves, only for spending a few months in the praised land? The historians rack their brains, but they do not dare to draw the obvious conclusions: They got hold of secret truths, scriptures and probably also land maps that totally rolled up the existing world view.

A copy of one of those secret old maps is publically known since the 16th century; it was discovered in Constantinople: The sensational Piri-Reis map that shows North America, South America and even the ice-free Antarctica besides Europe and Africa!"

The sudden appearance of the Templars
In 1118, Hugo de Payens, who was already 40 years old at that time, went on a fourth ride to Jerusalem. That time he was accompanied by eight chosen men - made up by famous knights and two Cistercian monks. Among the knights were people like the brother of the new king of Jerusalem (Balduin II) and the uncle of the legendary Bernhard, abbot

of the new Cistercian monastery of Clair-vaux. In Jerusalem, they set up their camp directly on the ground walls of Solomon's former temple, and that is where their first name, "The poor knights of Christ from the Solomonian temple in Jerusalem", originates, or, briefly, the Temple Knights/Templars.

It seemed as if these nine men had a special mission to fulfill because their main occupation was to do archaeological digging especially inside the temple mountain in Jerusalem as we nowadays have to assume. Legends go that in the year 70 A.D. secret artefacts had been buried there - shortly before the Romans destroyed the temple due to culminating riots. Nine years later a delegation of that group returned to France, led by Hugo de Payens and André de Montbard, the aforementioned uncle of the young but highly influential abbot of Clairvaux with the name Bernhard, who is today known as St. Bernhard of Clairvaux (1090–1153). That very man (André) was it, to immediately take the next steps. In early 1129, he convened the so-called synode of Troyes, where the Templar order was founded.

Gothic art and the sacred geometry

At that time, a breath-taking architectural activity also suddenly unfolded. Did the secret scriptures or teachings (and clairvoyant sources) also contribute to the discovery of sacred geometry, of the Sevenstar and Geomantics? In less than 150 years, between 1130 and 1260, about 80 fantastic churches and cathedrals were created simultaneously, for example in Paris (Notre-Dame), Strasbourg, Amiens, Rouen, Reims and Chartre; and shortly after those, others followed in other countries, of which the most famous are: Westminster Abbey in London (1245), the dome of Cologne (1248) and the dome

19

of Milano (1387). Many of these buildings were dedicated to Notre-Dame, "Our (dear) lady", and contained black madonnas. They were all built on very special locations that used to be sanctuaries since pagan times. At the beginning, the initiative and intelligence behind this intensive building activity came exclusively from the Templars and their patron order, the Cistercians. Under their guidance, unknown architects were working who stayed anonymous due to the job ethics of the time.

Those brilliant masters initially originated from a guild belonging to the Southern French Goths. This trace in turn guides us into the area of heretical philosophy that was secretly worshipped by Catharians and Templars. The anonymous master architects of Gothic art unfolded a completely new style of Sevenstar buildings with the help of the Templars' wealth and crew, which is accordingly called "Gothic art":

High-towering, double-towered buildings structured by shape that are flooded by light and charged with energy, which is even more surprising if we consider the fact that, beforehand, people used to build in Romanic style over centuries, meaning: bulky, heavy, austere and dark. The Gothic cathedrals are miracles of architecture, physics and statics and until today, 700 years later, they remain standing and are full of secrets. For example, there are conspicious parallels in the measurements of those cathedrals and the Gizeh pyramid! The cathedrals are built on power places, forming astrological constellations together with other sacred spots, especially the Virgo.

6. Setup of hives in Sevenstar

Soil intensity

While planning and setting up a stone circle, a Bee-Sevenstar or a rune exercising spot, the search for a suitable spot is an important prerequisite.

We know about water veins, grids, cubes and, for some time now, about the light grids from above. The surrounding soil is made up of various materials like rock, calcium, sand, humus and many others. All these units radiate a unique vibration (frequency, Hz) and energies working positively or negatively. All of this can be felt on that spot.

The interaction of all vibrations at a certain spot is called the soil intensity. This soil intensity can either be asked for spiritually or it can be measured via a soil intensity scale (similar to a Bovis scale).

The scale ranges from 0–100%. For setting up a Sevenstar or a stone circle, the soil intensity should have a minimum of 45%. After setting up an intact and fully occupied Bee-Sevenstar, it will rise up to 99% through the bees living there. But how can we find such a proper spot with an intensity of minimally 45% now? This has to be done via a spiritual technique:

You have to stand at the edge of the property in North-South direction and say the following sentence to the spiritual world:

„Show me the direction that has the best soil intensity on this property ahead of me for setting up a Bee-Sevenstar." The same has to be done again in East-West direction from the west edge (a divining rod may be used as helping tool for

21

people not capable of clairvoyant perception). The spot with the highest intensity will be where the two lines cross. If the spot is too close to the edge of the property to offer enough space for a Sevenstar so that it would be unavoidable to move the spots, you would have to ask for the spot with second highest intensity in that case.

A Bee-Sevenstar should be free of water veins, grids and cubes. If the space is not big enough under those conditions, the diameter of the Sevenstar can also be reduced to 6.5 metres. The entrances of the hives shall face outward.
First we draw a circle of 6.5 metres (or a multiple of 6.5) radius at the setup spot of our 7 bee colonies and mark the seven tips of the star on that circle (by choosing a first tip and then measuring a straight line of exactly 5.64 metres from that tip to the next point in the circle, as seen in the illustration below). On each of these seven spots we figured out we place a platform of approx. 40cms of height, and on those platforms we place our 7 bee colonies.

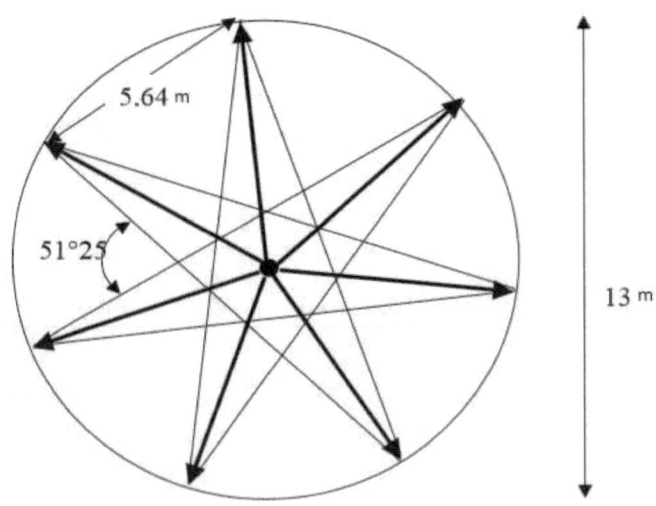

The angle between the chords towards the star tips is 51.25°, the circle of 360° divided with 7 makes approx. 51.42° and the slope angle of the great pyramid is approx. 51.8°, but these small differences are irrelevant for the Bee-Sevenstar.

This energy field is so powerful that all geopathogenic zones (like so-called Benkers, Hartmanns, Curries or effects of water veins) inside the effective area of the Sevenstar (a ball with 4.2 kilometres diameter) will annul their negative influences on all living beings. The vibration radiating from this new divine being, the bee-occupied Sevenstar, a vivid Stonehenge, is very valuable and important for the spiritual development of Mother Earth. Reverence and love overwhelm us as we think about these insights.

At the beginning, I had only four swarm colonies (on tips no. 1, 3, 4 and 5 of the star), I put a big stone to replace the fifth colony.

The diagram shows a Sevenstar, set up on 13th December 2006, with a diameter of 6.5 metres, a switch stone, a middle stone and only four bee colonies. For the 5th colony in the East I had to put a replacement stone (of course, it would be better to have all seven star tips occupied by a bee colony). Despite that, the entire place has already gotten a soil intensity of 99% in the meanwhile.

Hive no. 1 is moved by 6° towards NO to activate the Sevenstar:

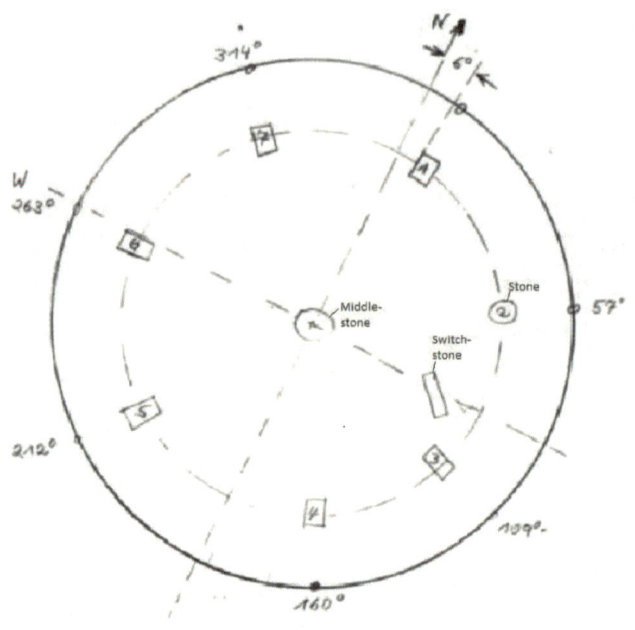

In 2006, I reckoned standard beekeepers honey to have approx. 3,000 Bovis units, Sevenstar honey to have approx. 8,000–15,000 Bovis units and Sevenstar honey from a Sevenstar that has four spiral antenna (in N,E,S,W directions) 20,000–90,000 units. The measurements proved my estimations to be correct. In the combination of Sevenstar and stone circle you can make use of the switch stone. Under every hive I have buried a rock of approx. 30kg weight. If the switchstone is placed on the E-W axis of the Sevenstone while facing from NW to SE direction (negatively charged, electrically speaking), it will affect the bees by calming them, to prevent them from flying out too early at the first warm days in spring. As soon as you change the switch stone in spring time, facing from SW to NE (positively charged), you will animate the bees and support them in their work.

Orientation of buildings, artefacts, natural formations and others on the NS-
and SE-magnetaxis and resulting energetic polarization

1)

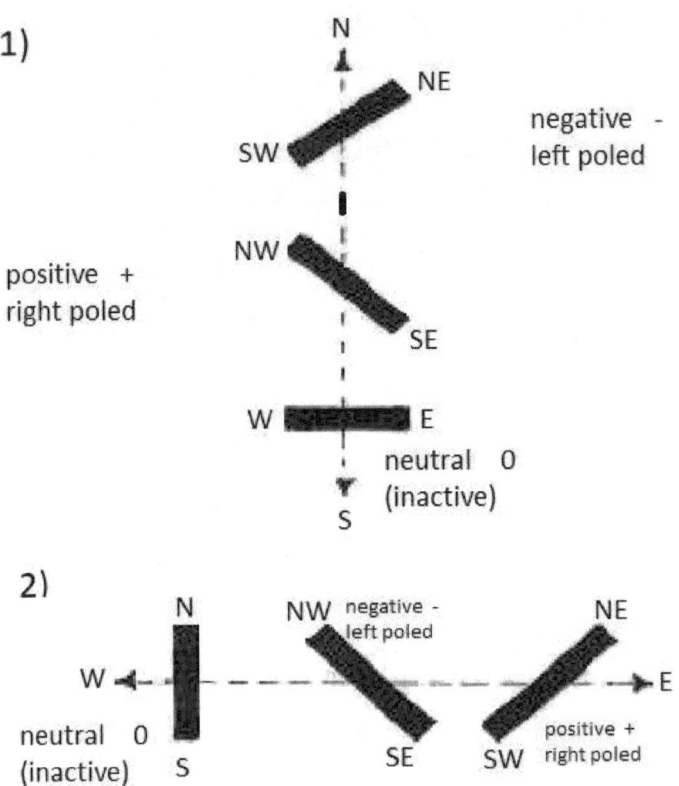

2)

Source: Erich Neumann p. 25

7

The "standing energy pillar"

"If water in a glass gets stirred fast enough with a spoon, a funnel is created in it. With that funnel, a 'standing energy pillar' (SEP) has formed. If stirred clockwise, it will be charged up with magnetic energy, its spin will become structured. If stirred counterclockwise, its spin will get chaotic, it will become unmagnetized." We know the SEP already from whirls in water and from wind vortexes. Our technicians work mostly with frequencies, ergo, with sinus waves; our ancestors had surprising successes with the SEP. They used it not only in technology; also, with the help of a SEP, a human was able to accelerate one's spiritual develop- ment. Heinrich Sannemann says that after the activation of the Bee-Sevenstar, the following happens:

"Above every colony that has a character of its own, a SEP will form that will direct cosmic energies from space into the colony. The Been transforms those energies and the powers of the Sevenstar will direct the transformed energies from all seven tips inwards to the centre (which correspond to the holy of holies in a cathedral). There they will be strenghtened and equally radiate in all directions, forming a ball from the centre. This 'ball' has a diameter of 4.2 kilometres in our latitudes, as explained before."

As we look at stone circles, we find the same proportions as in the Sevenstar. Bee-Sevenstars must not overlap each other with their effective zones of 4.2 kilometres, otherwise the effects we explained before will be undone. Thus, the distance towards the next Sevenstar has to be at least 2.1

kilometres. But stone circles can be set up directly next to the Bee-Sevenstar without impeding each other.

In nature, every stone has got a purpose. On the very spot where it is lying, its mass affects the energy field of the Earth, and be it only a tiny bit. Erich Neumann has described his very detailed research on stone circles with five and more stones and their effects in his book *Feinkrafttechnik*. According to his book, above every stone circle that has been set up properly, an enormous SEP forms, comparable to Stonehenge in South England, for example. The next illustration (done by E. Neumann) shows a stone circle of reduced size in which the energy flows radiate strongly in all directions, even though a heel pillar is missing. The same radiance forms above a vivid Sevenstar occupied by approx. 300,000 bees with even more power. This energy field is so strong that even the negative influences of all geopathogenic zones (e.g. grids, Benkers and water veins) on living beings inside the effective zone of the Sevenstar will be cancelled. I have checked that radius using a distance counter for bicycles.
Again we are overwhelmed by reverence and love as we think about these insights on stone circles.

I repeat, every bee colony with a naturally grown queen has got a „standing energy pillar" that is absorbing cosmic energies out of space and passing them on to Mother Earth, and that effect is multiplied in colonies standing in a Sevenstar setup. In winter, every beekeeper can observe the bees forming a winter cluster with the queen inside the protected, warm centre of it. At the time of the twelve sacred nights in winter that cluster opens up and forms a double barbell, leaving the queen completely open and unprotected in the centre at the night of 31st December. All worker bees rotate around her in double-eight-movements (like the infinity symbol) to absorb and save a maximum of cosmic energies for the following year. By midnight time of 6th December (Epiphany day) the cluster around the queen is closed again completely. From then on, the bees climb from bottom to top inside the cluster; once they reach the top they move back down on the cold outside. Thus, the 12 days and nights before are the actual time of regeneration of our bees which are otherwise busy 24 hours a day.

The following excerpt is from B. Chales-de Beaulieu's book *Der vergessene Schritt*:

"For the turning phases to the left and the right at both ends of the ellipse the earth needs 12 days between 15th to 26th of December and 15th to 26th of June. Because no acceleration forces are required in those end phases of the cycle, cosmic energies become free and available for all vivid beings on earth. It takes nine days for those energies to reach the earth. That is why the 24th December and the 24th June mark the

The elliptical path of the earth around the sun:

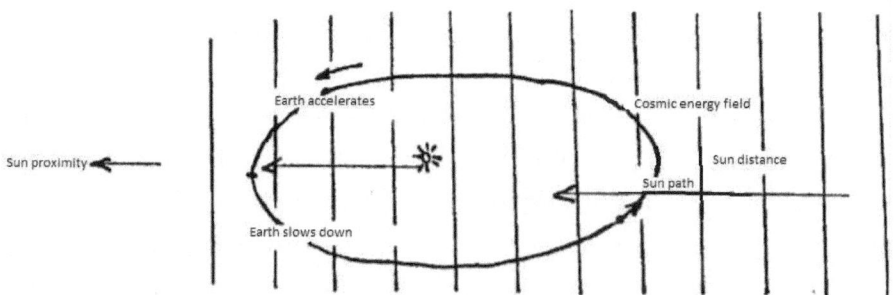

beginning of the twelve-day period of cosmic energy recharge of all vivid beings."

The tips of the Sevenstar direct all energies to the centre and from there, like rays of sunlight, into all directions. Thus, the radiation works not only to the side but also into the atmosphere and into the soil, and that is exactly what makes it so important for Mother Earth. But it will take 26 hours after the fifth swarm colony is placed on the star tips until the energies start to flow.

Those energy flows can be felt even by a medium sensitive human as you step out of the stars' centre as well as at the entrance of the hives on the star tips. In order for those energy flows not to be disturbed, no vegetation should grow inside the Sevenstar that is between 30cms and 160cms in height (like nettles, silybum marianum, etc.). Stems of trees whose branches start at 160cm or above are **not** disturbing.

Combining a stone circle and a Bee-Sevenstar by placing seven stones below the hive boxes will increase the energy even further. For that, you should look for seven rocks that are of elongated shape and of approximately the same size, up to 50kgs of weight. If space is limited, the stones below the hives can also be buried completely in the soil. If doing so, it is recommended to place them alternately with one having the thicker side (minus –) facing downwards and the next one facing upwards.

In ancient stone circles (e.g. Stonehenge in South England) minus pole and plus pole take turns, too. The stones in our Sevenstar should stand vertically. If one uses almost round stones, the proper polarity will set in automatically.

This process increases the energy by another 25%. An elongated rock of about 10kgs of weight is placed as a switchstone either in NS-direction or EW-direction (depending on the effect that is wished for, as explained before).

Every change that is done to the hives or the stones, even adding additional empty hive boxes (meaning before all 7 tips are occupied), and even leaving a wheelbarrow there would **change** the energy relations. That is why the space inside the Sevenstar must **never** be changed once it has been set up (except for removing plants that would disturb, as explained before).

As you are closing the lid of the hive, be especially careful **not** to mash even a single bee. This would be an offence against the divine law of the Bee-Sevenstar. One has to communicate with the hives' spirit to order the single bee back into the comb. If that does not work, smoke may be used to help. One must **never** kill a bee intentionally or collaterally! And, of course, **never** kill a queen bee, no matter whatever the circumstances are!

8

How can the Sevenstar be effective with less than five colonies?

If one of the five colonies passes away in the same year in which the Sevenstar was built, the energy will drop and the star will lose its potential. If the fifth colony passes away after the sacred night of the winter solstice, the potential of the star will remain active even with only four colonies. If only four swarm colonies are available in the beginning, the fifth can be replaced by a rock of 10–50kgs of weight.

How to make the Sevenstar active with a mix of colonies with bred queens and swarm queens:

If a Sevenstar is built with colonies being partly swarm-queen-led and partly breed-queen-led, having less than five swarm-colonies, the star will not radiate outwards yet. The increasing energy will flow from the centre into the hives, but inside some hives it will be blocked because of the bred queen lacking an individual character. But in a process of 16 hours, the energy of the breed queen and her colony will increase more and more until the flow of energy can return into the centre without hindrance; and from that moment on, the Sevenstar starts to radiate.

Unfortunately, that can be a lethal problem for breed queens. If the beekeeper puts a breed-queen-led colony directly into an active Sevenstar without preparation, the breed queen and her workers will not be able to tolerate the sudden increase of energy. They would leave the hive or, if you tried to hinder them, they would die. The same happens to the Varroa mite, as we will explain later in detail. Thus, the breed queen and her colony have to be prepared first.

How to increase the energy of a breed queen to the level of a swarm queen:

It may happen that we do not have enough swarm colonies to be put in the Sevenstar. So I want to explain two possibilities of how to raise the energy of a breed queen here, without having to wait for the development of new queen cups. **First,** however, I have to say most clearly that this is only to be practised in case of emergency! **Nothing** can replace a real swarm colony!

1) To form an artificial "swarm", you may take any breed queen, ideally from a strong colony having natural queen cups. Otherwise, any breed queen has to make do. Add worker bees to that queen, again, ideally from a strong colony, otherwise from various colonies. If queen and workers come from different colonies, the queen has to be protected by a cage for the beginning phase. This artificial "swarm" needs to be put into an empty hive box equipped with a grid to keep the bees inside and with enough food and water for some days (food:water = 50:50). Keep that box in the cellar or another place properly protected from sun. In any case, wherever you put it, make sure the bees get enough air to breathe properly; otherwise they might overheat.

Now, what will happen in that colony? We call that process "harmonization", but it is actually an increase of energy taking place during that resting period. In about 70 hours the chemistry inside the queen's body will change enough for an increase of her energy taking place at the end of the process in the last 30 minutes. This will also happen in the bodies of

33

the worker bees. The cause of this miraculous energy increase is the fact that the nature of bees always seeks to return to its roots.

2) The second option to raise energy requires an active Bee-Sevenstar (e.g. the one of a beekeeper friend). One may take a colony from any location, put the bred queen into a protection cage and tie the loaded cage to a branch fixed directly in the centre of a Sevenstar. Then you have to shake or hit the closed hive box with the colony in it because that will stimulate the bees inside to fill their stomachs with honey. There after, brush about half of the bees off the combs, next to the branch with the queen. Put the rest of the hive back into its original place. The bees you brushed away will gather around the queen in cluster shape, but since the queen is in her cage, the swarm cannot fly away.
The centre of the Sevenstar has not got as much energy as the tips, it is only about the amount a breed queen can still tolerate. After 16 hours the colony can be moved into a new hive. Subsequently, it will act like a swarm colony in all regards. The process was a simulated act of swarming. Now, this colony can be put on a star tip. It has still got the same queen; no transfer from a queen cup had to be done.

If an active Sevenstar is available, the 70 hours as explained in 1) can be reduced to 16 hours by placing the hive in the centre of the Sevenstar. The proof that these energies really affect the bees as explained will follow immediately: After placing the hive in the centre, suddenly the bees will start to walk around and cool the brood more frequently. That is why fresh air has to be brought in via open grids at the **top and bottom** of the box; otherwise our darlings would most definitely **die from overheating**. The transformation will then take place in the centre of the Sevenstar, as in the "swarm cluster" I talked about before.

The Sevenstar technique

Every beekeeper should actually try to work only with natural swarming. That way the bees will get their original energy back. Due to our queen breeding, artificial insemination and other unnatural practices, the bees degenerate and would finally withdraw from our Earth, i.e., they extinct themselves via the diseases already spreading today. Without the Sevenstar protection wall we can preserve our darlings only by killing the drone brood, which contains most of the mites, and by using strong poisons to kill those mites. In every jar of honey coming from non-Sevenstar beekeeping the poisons used are found in small quantities. **Sevenstar honey is demonstrably without poisonous remnants from mite fighting because they are not required in this technique.** If Varroa mites do appear, the combs would be sprayed only with "Brottrunk", the same way as the conventional beekeeper would use formic acid. "Brottrunk" (literally: bread drink) is a beverage made by fermenting integral flour bread in water, similar to the slavic "bread kvass" that is used as a probiotic to support human health. Its taste is slightly sour and it is often sweetened with honey before consumed. Thus, it can also be used during the time of honey collection, even during the breeding time, without causing harm to the bees.

The Bovis scale

The Bovis scale was developed by the French physicist André Bovis. The scale describes the intensity of an energetic stimulus. It is a linear scale with units named "bio-angström" by its developer; Nowadays, they are simply named "Bovis units". The value 0 was set by Bovis as "death", most likely because a dead being does not radiate any life energies. A healthy newborn's radiation was fixed as the value of 6,500 units. The top of the scale is unlimited. For example, the water of the sacred spring of Lourdes in South France has got 11,000 units. A sacred energy line, often referred to as "Leyline" in geomantics, usually radiates between 40,000 and 80,000 units. Anything below the "neutral value" of 6,500 is dismantling energy, like almost all water veins, unfortunately. Anything above is positive and builds up energy, e.g. leylines, electric pluspoles or growth lines. If the scale does not go far enough in a measurement, you start all over again and add the results together, or you may use a logarithmic scale as found in old slide rules, or you may work mentally without using any scale.

If a spot's value lies below 3,000 Bovis, it is called a cancer spot, meaning it is cancerogenic in the long run. The Bovis scale is only to be used by experts on the topic and in combination with divining rod, pendulum or tensor. **Thus, we are not talking about physically measurable values here; it is a spiritual scale.**

Now someone could get the idea that all spots below a value of 6,500 were bad. That is not the case. Not all spots with a value above 6,500 are good, either. It is actually quite obvious why that is a fact: If you are in chronic fatigue, you need a strongly positive spot (like an electric pluspole) to recharge yourself. If you are hyperactive, you need a negative spot (like a minuspole) to calm yourself down. It is all relative. Bovis units in the minus zone also exist. That is why

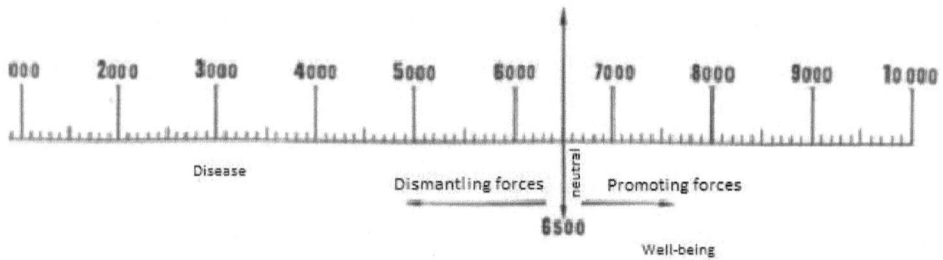

Biometer of A. **Bovis** (Physicist)

replenished by SIMONETON (engineer)

SCALE FOR DISCERNMENT OF HUMAN RADIATION (vitality) and LOCATIONS (local energetic condition)

the scale in the chart continues to the left.

Some natural laws of handling bees, as described by Mathias K. Thun in his book *"Die Biene. Haltung und Pflege"*, are also recommended for the Sevenstar-beekeeper:

In early spring, when sun and Venus stand before the sign of Aquarius, the first cleansing flight will start. Some days before, bird protection nets and mouse protection grids should be removed so that our darlings have free access to the entrance. A regularly checked inlay is very useful in spring to reckon the amount of used honey, using as indicator the amount of wax lids that have been removed from the combs and dropped onto the inlay. Dead drones indicate that the colony has breed a new queen recently and the old queen did not make it to her nuptial flight. If the beekeeper finds the bees walking around the entrance on the day of the cleansing flight, looking like searching for something, they did not manage to create new queen cups and the beekeeper may help that colony.

In the first period of Venus standing before Aquarius, poplar, hazel and alder trees offer their pollen. This time is suitable for uniting queen-cup-less colonies with others. Mathias K. Thun wrote that he was able to observe the works of the bees in relation to the moon cycle very clearly:

As the moon passes Aries, Leo and Sagittarius, more nectar is collected. As she passes Gemini, Libra and Aquarius, pollen collection is stimulated and Taurus, Virgo and Capricornus stimulate the building activity.

A beautifully designed Bee-Sevenstar with a diameter of 13 metres, created by Rupert Peterlechner in St. Radegont, Austria

39

According to *Die Aussaattage* by Maria Thun, the following times are favorable:

Jobs to be done on the colony in early spring or offspring creation on light/flower days when Moon passes Gemini, Libra or Aquarius.

No disturbance of the colony is to be done on water/leaf days when Moon passes Pisces, Cancer or Scorpio (stinging impulse of the bees is stronger then).

Colony checks in early summer, formation of artificial swarms on fire/fruit days, as Moon passes Aries, Leo or Sagittarius because then the bees are especially peaceful.

Moving in of an artificial swarm or building activity is favorable on earth/root days when the moon passes Taurus, Capricornus or Virgo.

Swarming is stimulated when Venus or Mars pass before Taurus. As soon as at least one queen cup is covered with its lid, they can start to swarm.

Less honey removal from the "sacred bees"?

Due to one of the aims of this Sevenstar beekeeping style being the effect on the planet Earth, the flora and fauna as well as on the human, I remove only the part of honey from those "sacred bees" that they will definitely will not need for the winter. For every two jambs, they should be left with 18–20kg of honey. The bees on the Sevenstar need more food than normal bees because they have to keep a higher temperature of 40.5°C instead of 34.5°C for their brood.

The specific life cycle on the Bee-Sevenstar

The colonies of a heptagram can mostly be left alone as "sacred bees". They regenerate, grow and die. **They should be disturbed as little as possible.**

If a swarm was captured, another young queen would be raised and the old queen be poisoned by twelve bees of her state. She will not be stung to death as usually because it seems that would be an offence against the bees' special ethics in the Sevenstar.

Thus, the only jobs to be done on those colonies are:

a) Cleansing and changing of combs every 2 years.

b) Creating the necessary space for expansion of the colony by adding another box if it is needed.

c) The Sevenstar colonies need a huge variety of flowers. If there are not enough left in the immediate surroundings, honey must be fed, possibly even in the middle of season.

d) Combs of colonies that passed away have to be melted down. New colonies should not be furnished with the frames typically used that have got wire on them (even though that will definitely make the "harvest" more difficult).

e) If a colony is in the mood for swarming, the queen will show that the evening before by making noises. Around noon time the following day, all bees will suddenly fly back into the hive to pick up honey for the swarm flight. That is the right moment to set up the swarm-catching sack. Immediately after that, the bees will swarm with rumble into the sack (catching swarms, of course, should only be practised until you have your seven colonies for the heptagram). The remaining honey inside the hive should remain inside the hive for the rest of the colony.

Sevenstar-honey with 100,000 Bovis units, coming from a Sevenstar-beekeper in Monsheim/Worms (Germany).
Compared to that, a typical Langnese honey from the supermarket has about 750 Bovis units. Similarly, self-baked bread or salad from one's own garden is far higher in energy. That is why people should be careful about what they eat.

11

What happens to the Varroa on the bee heptagram?

Since 2004, the bees in Ratingen have been standing in the Sevenstar. Due to that, the vibration energy of the bees increased so much that a harmonic coexistence of the two populations (i.e. our darlings, the bees, and the Varroa mite) became impossible. The Varroa have left these colonies voluntarily!

After being set up in the Sevenstar, the bees remained free of the parasite through the entire season until the honey theft in fall time. The same experience is made here with the mites as with the bred queens, which, once put on the Sevenstar, will either fly away or die. Varroa mites also die or emigrate elsewhere.

Another possibility to reduce the numbers of mites on our darlings' backs, without using poisons, can be found in the teachings of Rudolf Steiner: incineration of the Varroa.

Mathias Thun has described this very illustratively in his book *Die Biene, Haltung und Pflege*. In this method, a spoonful of Varroa mites are incinerated in a closed oven at the right astrological time, using beech wood. The ashes have to be grinded in a porcelain mortar for a minimum of one hour until resulting in a fine dust.

That dust is then spread over the infected combs at the right time, using a salt shaker, for example. The content of a normal, small salt shaker should be enough for about 25 colonies of bees.

According to M. Thun, the right time is when sun and moon stand in the sign of Taurus. If there is a solar eclipse in that period, the incineration should be done shortly before the peak of the eclipse. Many experiments of his have shown that the life-inhibiting effects are strongest shortly before the peak of a solar eclipse. That is not necessary, though, as it just increases the ashes' power, but the sun and moon positions _must_ be as explained before.

The right time to apply the ashes on the hive can be either when the moon stands in Taurus or, even better, when sun and moon both stand in Taurus. The treatment has to be done three times; only then you can be sure of optimal effects. Up to now, M. Thun can tell definitely from his experiments that the best effects have been seen when the incineration and the first application are done while sun and moon both stand in Taurus; the second application may be carried out four weeks later as the moon returns into Taurus and, another four weeks later, the third application may take place. The second and the third application do not necessarily require the sun in Taurus, either, but incineration and first treatment should have both sun and moon standing in Taurus.

My Bee-Sevenstar in Ratingen, Germany, using beech stems as base. Those stems can be equipped with glue rings for defense against ants.

Like in homeopathy, spiritual forces contribute to this technique. In the thriving process of a bee colony, the love and care of the beefather always decides about woe or welfare of his colonies.

The actual primeval form is the octagon, the divine cause of all existence. Thus, the heptagram as we know, is not complete. The eighth element, as we can see it in the flower of life, is missing:

45

The flower of Life

So, where is the eighth tip of the star to be found? In the spiritual world, all forms can possibly be thought of. Thus, the eighth tip of the star can also be found virtually in the centre.

It is the beemother or the beefather who is the most important component of the Been. Without her/him, there would be no bee in the heptagram:

Source: Wikipedia

46

As you can see in this image, the old Templars back in their days had already put the human in the centre. The alchemist heptagram containing the vitriol formula shows the human face in the centre to which the hands and feet belong that are seen on the left and right.

These four limbs point to the four elements: The right hand holds a torch (fire), the left hand holds the bladder of a fish (air), the right foot is standing on the earth and the left on the sea (water). The fifth element (ether) is represented by the Hermes symbol (double wing) crowning the heptagram. These five element symbols are structured in the shape of a regular pentagram. Next to the feet, king (sun) and queen (moon) are sitting, with the symbols of sun and moon on their crowns, to encode the bipolar forces of nature. Further, the picture shows two more objects: a triangle and a circle. The triangle carries the Latin words "corpus", "anima" and "spiritus" on its corners, thus representing the trinity of body, soul and mind, or, speaking in alchemist terms: Sal (= body, the solidified principle), Sulfur (= soul, the moving principle), Mercurius (= spirit, the mediating principle).

As soon as the beemother/-father has _understood_ this, the bees entrusted to them will thrive and become real "power plants" of energy able to contribute massively to the _help and healing_ of Mother Earth.

If we add an equilateral cross as well as a vertical and horizontal infinity symbol to this flower of life, our thoughts move into the spiritual plane and we learn to understand why Christmas and summer solstice time are so important for us and the bees.

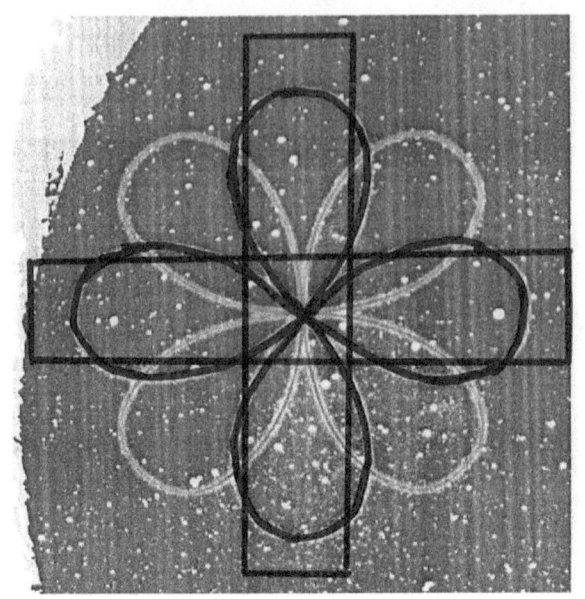

12

Use the Sevenstar instead of poison!

Often the environment is blamed for diseases and the death of the bees. However, if they were treated according to their own nature, the majority of these existing weaknesses would be reduced.

All we need to do is to emotionally tune in to the character of our darlings, the bees, and we will learn to understand their behaviour, and why it does not make sense to use force when trying to solve the problem.

The Sevenstar is an ideal tool to free bee colonies from the Varroa mite. A colony which needs treatment is first set into the centre of the heptagram for 12 hours for the purpose of harmonization. I repeat how important it is to make sure air can enter from above and below to keep them from overheating. After those 12 hours you can close the entrance of a colony standing on a star tip and remove it from there for a short while.

The varroa-infected colony can now (after locking its entrance also) be put on the free spot on the star tip. After seven hours, the vast majority of Varroa mites will have escaped or died. Seven hours are enough, even for the breeding combs to be cleaned. After this process, both colonies can be put back into their original positions and the locks on the entrances can be removed. Swarm-queen colonies can even be put directly onto a star tip. The bee-heptagram serves the purposes of Varroa fighting as well as helping Mother Earth to survive. With more and more Sevenstars set up in a distance of 2.1 kilometres, all Earth could be harmonized covering the needs.

The following charts clearly prove the devastating effect the Sevenstar has on the Varroa:

In the Sevenstar colonies I did not have any notable problems with the Varroa until August/September of 2007 as the weekly check of the inlay in the hives proved. That August/September 2007, my neighbouring beekeeper set up three new colonies that were heavily infected. He did not do anything about it at the time because he only realized the problem about 4–6 weeks later when he was astonished not to find any honey nor any bees left in his hives. Ever since that beekeeper has become my neighbour, I keep on getting minor problems with mites from time to time. Especially in 2007, my Sevenstar colonies suddenly got infected, too, in particular colony no. 4, with up to 2000 mites per week after many years without any problems.

My bees had brought them in while robbing the neighbours' colonies. In the charts, one can see the development of mites very clearly and in contrast to the colonies ABC that stood outside of the Sevenstar. That is the power of the Sevenstar!

Varroa-inlay-statistics of 7 Heptagram-colonies and 3 economical colonies (ABC) which stood only 50 metres away

(kg=honey yield / T=Thymol-Apilife Var Treatment)
Evaluation 07   Ratingen, 09.12.2007

Colony	1	2	3	4	5	6	7	A	B	C
10.03.07	0	2	6	4	4	1		2	3	2
17.03.	0	2	0	6	5	0		3	4	2
24.03.	0	2	0	0	0	0		1	0	0
31.03.	0	1	1	0	0	0		0	0	0
06.04.	0	0	1	0	1	1		0	0	0
12.04.	0	0	0	1	0	0		0	0	0
20.04.	1	0	0	0	0	0		0	0	0
27.04.	0	0	0	0	0	1		0	0	0
05.05.	0	0	0	1	0	2		0	0	0
12.05.	0	1	0	1	0	0		0	0	1
19.05.	11kg....0	30kg...0	15kg....0	18kg...1	0	22kg...0		43kg....1	0	1
26.05.	0	0	0	0	0	0		0	0	0
03.06.	0	0	0	0	-	0		0	0	1
18.06.	0	0	0	0	-	0		0	0	2
25.06.	0	0	0	0	-	0		0	0	5
02.07.	0	3	0	1	0	0		4	0	2
09.07.	0	0	0	5	0	-		45kg...2	0	2
16.07.	21kg...0	22kg...0	0	21kg...18	0	-		2	31kg...0	45kg...3
23.07.	4	4	3	26	2	1		1	18	5
30.07.	4	4	4	30	2	-	Offspring	3	16	37
08.08.	40	16	25	120	10	0		-	28	29
15.08.	8	8	4	T...206	5	3		T...6	T...108	T...151
22.08.	12	39	18	2118	5	2		38	219	312
30.08.	20	T...41	T....35	1261	T...36	3		18	42	581
16.09.	19	156	T...115	T...166	118	1		96	5	116
21.09.	T...18	T...242	251	85	146	-		-	-	103
02.10.	861	155	386	49	118	41	T...0	T...92	T...21	T.....-
26.10.	1086	206	121	54	121	38	4	104	8	91
02.11.	6	3	84	3	0	0	18	6	0	5
09.11.	8	0	0	0	0	0	0	1	1	3
15.11.	0	0	0	0	0	0	1	0	0	0

Varroa-inlay-statistics of 7 Heptagram-colonies and 3 economical colonies (ABC) which stood only 50 metres away

(kg=honey yield / T=Thymol-Apilife Var-Treatment / B="Bienenwohl"-BR Brottrunk Treatment)
Evaluation 2008   Ratingen, 07.01.2009

Volk	1	2	3	4	5	6	7	A	B	C
16.02.08	0	0	0	0	0	0	0	0	0	0
23.02.	0	0	0	0	0	0	0	0	0	0
29.02.	0	0	0	0	0	0	0	0	0	0
07.03.	0	0	0	0	0	0	0	0	0	0
14.03.	0	0	0	0	0	0	0	0	0	0
21.03.	0	0	0	0	0	0	0	0	0	0
28.03.	0	0	0	0	0	0	0	1	0	0
04.04.	0	0	0	0	0	2	0	0	0	0
11.04.	0	0	0	0	0	10	0	0	0	0
18.04.	0	0	0	0	1	12	0	0	0	0
25.04.	4	0	0	0	BR 0	11	0	0	1	0
02.05.	3	0	0	BR 0	BR 5	10	0	0	1	0
09.05.	1	0	0	BR 0	3	5	0	0	1	0
16.05.	0	0	0	0	8	2	0	0	1	0
23.05.	0	0	0	0	1	0	0	0	27kg 0	0
1.05.	0	0	0	0	1	0	0	0	1	0
07.06.	4kg 0	0	9kg 0	10kg 0	0	0	0	0	0	0
14.06.	0	0	0	0	0	0	2	0	0	0
21.06.	0	0	0	0	0	1	0	0	0	0
28.06.	2	0	0	2	BR 5	2	0	0	1	0
05.07.	3	0	18kg 0	10kg 1	18	5	1	0	32kg 1	0
10.07.	8	0	0	1	17	5	0	0	0	0
19.07.	5	1	0	1	13	1	0	0	0	0
27.07.	2	0	0	4	19	0	0	0	1	0
03.08.	2	0	0	6	86	5	0	1	2	0
09.08.	16kg 15	10kg 0	0	5kg 18	101	T9	0	0	4	0
16.08.	T 163	13kg 0	0	T 91	T 110	T 74	4kg 0	0	4	0
26.08.	31	5	11	86	323	88	0	0	9	1
29.08.	61	4	12	65	821	71	1	0	7	2
09.09.	24	0	T 68	T 59	T 986	T 26	0	0	T 63	T 4
16.09.	122	12	186	123	821	18	T 0	0	T 71	75
23.09.	36	56	156	113	71	21	23	0	T 126	T 11
30.09.	31	84	192	95	48	17	15	0	110	162
07.10.	16	72	85	84	47	13	8	0	93	110
14.10.	20	11	T 63	26	21	1	8	0	T 84	74
21.10.	25	10	25	18	4	2	19	12	25	86
28.10.	28	3	20	9	2	1	10	58	19	23

04.11.	12	7	25	34	6	3	19	23	20	12
11.11.	6	12	41	26	6	2	4	12	18	13
20.11.	10	3	22	15	5	0	6	31		
27.11.	28	11	12	9	0	0	4	12	6	20
03.12.	22	12	8	7	0	3	5	31	3	9
10.12.	11	8	8	8	0	0	0	29	0	8
17.12.	B 45	B 25	B 19	B 10	0	1	B 2	B 35	0	B 8
24.12.	21	64	21	53	0	0	18	162	0	9
31.12.	15	14	5	18	0	0	5	41	0	2
05.01.09	8	5	4	4	0	0	3	4	0	0

Varroa-inlay-statistics of 7 Heptagram-colonies and 3 economical colonies (ABC) which stood only 50 metres away

(kg=honey yield / T=Thymol-Apilife-Var-Treatment / E=Honey fed back to bees)
Evaluation 2009   Ratingen, 07.12.09

Colony	1	2	3	4	5	6	7	A	B	C
05.04.09	0	0	0	0	0	0	0	0	0	0
12.04.	1	0	0	0	0	0	0	1	0	0
19.04.	0	0	0	0	0	0	0	0	0	0
26.04.	1	0	0	0	1	0	0	1	0	0
03.05.	1	0	0	0	0	0	0	0	0	0
10.05.	1	0	0	0	0	0	0	1	0	0
14.05.	15kg 0	35kg 0	15kg 0	4kg 3	0	0	0	1	0	25kg 0
24.05.	0	0	0	2	0	0	0	0	0	0
01.06.	0	0	0	0	1	0	0	0	0	0
08.06.	0	0	0	0	1	0	0	1	0	0
15.06.	0	0	0	0	0	0	0	0	1	0
22.06.	3	0	2	1	1	0	0	0	1	0
29.06..	1	0	0	1	0	0	0	0	1	0
06.07.	2	0	0	2	0	0	0	0	3	0
13.07.	0	0	0	1	0	0	0	1	0	0
20.07.	0	0	1	1	0	0	0	0	1	22kg 1
27.07.	22kg 1	10kg 0	9kg 2	6kg 0	0	0	16kg 0	0	0	0
03.08.	1	0	3	2	0	0	2	0	3	2
10.08.	0	0	1	0	8	1	0	1	5	2
17.08.	0	0	3	2	10	2	0	1	8	2
24.08.	13kgE 0	10kgE 1	18kgE 0	16kgE 1	13kE 18	18kgE 0	13kgE 1	2	10	4
31.08.	0	0	15	27	17	25	0	1	23	16
07.09.	29	1	19	18	T 86	31	0	14kgE 8	18	12kE20
14.09.	4	0	8	T 24	369	T 66	0	7	14kgE22	T 51
20.09.	20	5	T 31	768	556	896	0	T 5	T 582	910
28.09.	15	4	566	482	265	294	0	246	564	3kZ622
08.10.	25	9	210	186	110	93	4kg 0	182	266	125
15.10.	31	0	111	108	96	61	0	111	191	8
22.10.	15	0	82	65	61	44	1	84	105	0
29.10.	11	0	66	54	22	22	0	60	84	0
05.11.	31	0	28	23	9	0	T 0	41	16	5
12.11.	30	0	20	20	2	0	23	39	8	0
	50kg	55kg	42kg	26kg	13kg	18kg	33kg	14kg	14kg	59kg
									total	324kg
									Average	32,4kg

Varroa-inlay-statistics of 7 Heptagram-colonies and 3 economical colonies (ABC) which stood only 50 metres away

(kg=honey yield / T=Thymol-Apilife Var Treatment / E=honey fed back to bees)
Evaluation 2010   Ratingen, 07.12.2010

Volk	1	2	3	4	5	6	7	A	B	C
05.04.10	0		1	5	2				2	
12.04.	0		0	0	1				1	
19.04.	0		0	0	0				0	
26.04.	0		0	0	0				0	
03.05.	0		0	1	0				0	
10.05.	0		0	0	0				0	
14.05.	0		0	0	0	0	1	0	0	
24.05.	0		1	0	0	0	1	0	0	
01.06.	0		0	0	0	0	0	0	0	
08.06.	0		0	0	0	0	0	0	0	
15.06.	8kg 0		6kg 0	18kg 0	0	0	0	1	20kg 0	
22.06.	0		0	0	0	0	0	0	5	
29.06..	0		2	2	1	0	0	0	2	
06.07.	0	T	0	0	0	0	0	0	3	
13.07.	0	41	0	0	0	0	0	1	0	
20.07.	0	36	0	0	0	0	0	1	3	
27.07.	0	25	0	0	0	0	0	0	4	
03.08.	#	20	3	1	0	0	0	2	#	
10.08.	#	18	#	2	1	1	0	0	#	T 5
17.08.	#	8	#	0	0	#	0	5	0	22
24.08.	#	5	#	1	1	#	0	5	0	28
31.08.	20kg#	15kg 0	22kg 0	42kg 2	17kg 1	24kg #	6kg 0	24kg 8	43kg 8	65
07.09.	T#	T 0	3	T 31	3	0	T 15	T 5	T 42	T 144
14.09.	#	0	3	340	0	0	T 16	7	240	189
20.09.	#	0	12	120	0	0	22	9	231	96
28.09.	#	0	T 56	T 128	0	0	31	195	226	64
08.10.	2	1	68	75	4	2	65	190	205	76
15.10.	2	2	T 71	61	3	3	50	T 88	191	52
22.10.	3	1	92	45	5	2	44	56	116	41
29.10.	3	8	96	16	3	5	32	45	54	35
05.11.	0	4	122	4	2	4	24	41	41	30
12.11.	4	0	106	9	3	3	8	39	13	4
19. Nov	3	1	104	0	0	8	3	19	6	2
27. Nov	0	0	56	1	1	6	4	8	5	0
	28kg	15kg	30kg	60kg	17kg	24kg	8kg	24kg	63kg	3kg
				total	280kg	28kg per colony				

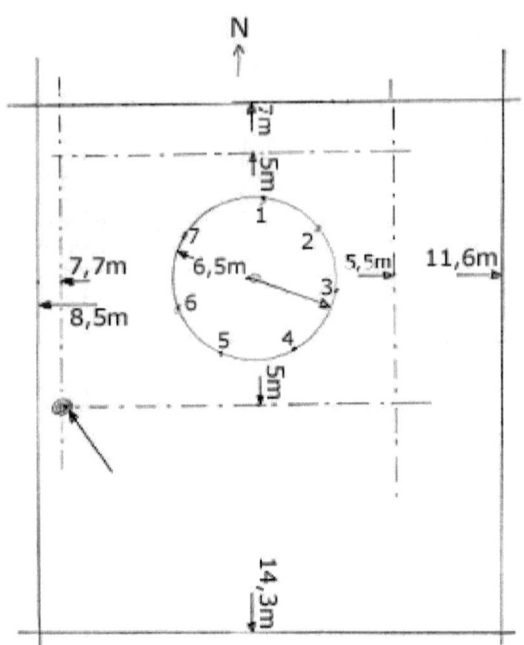

The main task of the Sevenstar is to harmonize the earth and anul the disease-bringing effects of hidden radiations (like water veins). If your Sevenstar stands on a good spot and is activated, the earth will be harmonized in a diameter of 4.2 kilometres.

(A Bee-Sevenstar, as explained before, should not stand on a "benker" grid, which is a geomantic term for radiation grids that come out of the earth, usually in a square of 10×10 metres. A benker stream can be moved out of the designated Sevenstar setup spot using a heavy stone.)

In my area, the benkers were also 10×10 metres wide, so I could not give my Sevenstar a 13-metre diameter without overlapping with them. In the southwest, exactly on the corner of two benker streams meeting, I put a rock of approx.

30kg weight and, immediately, the benker increased its size to 17×21 metres.

The graphic below shows the old benker grid size (broken line) and the new size after putting the stone on its corner (continuous line).

Additionally, four double-spiral antenna have been put up in N,E,S,W in a radius of 8.5 metres for further magnification of the vibrations (the @ in the graphic below).

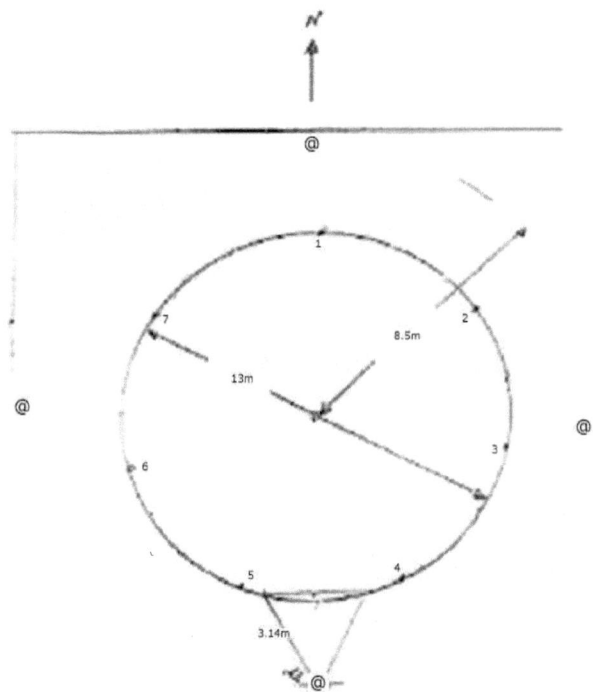

Beside the divine number _nine_ (2×9 = 18), we find the natural angle of 51.2° in our Sevenstar, between the hive spots and the central stone. This is the same angle as in the _pyramids_ in Gizeh, Egypt. Additionally, you can see the triangle between the circle and the spiral antenna being set up in a way that its sides are *3.14m (Pi)* long. Due to this precise placement and the additional four spiral antenna, its effective radius is not the normal 4.2kms but *9.2kms instead.*

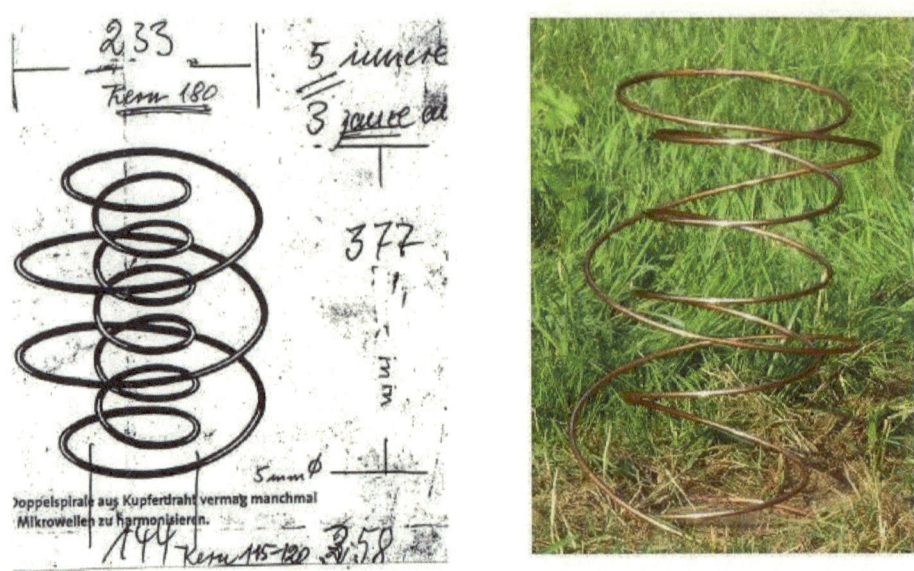

Double spiral antenna
made from copper wire

In that circle of 9.2 kms the Bee-Sevenstar helps *Mother Earth* to defend herself against the many, many environmental sins that fall onto her committed by man. Additionally, it *cancels* the *damaging* influences of benker grids and water veins. Whoever works or lives inside this circle will not get any *cancers, MS, stomach problems or osteoporosis.*

Biophysical Bovis units of the Bee Sevenstar
measured on 1st of July, 2009

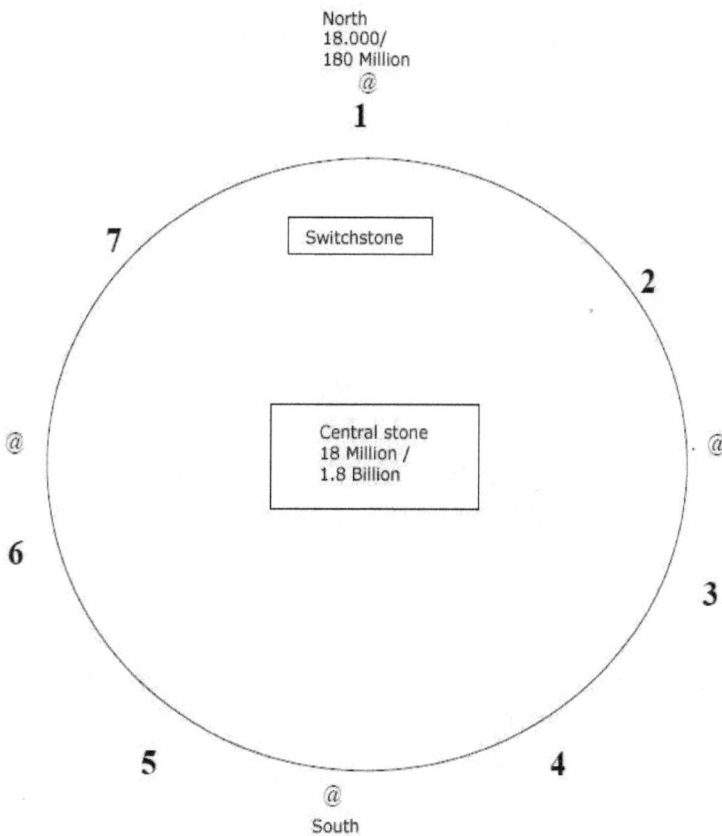

North
18.000/
180 Million
@

1

Switchstone

7

2

@

Central stone
18 Million /
1.8 Billion

@

6

3

5

4

@
South

@ Four double spiral antenna in N,E,S,W

Near all seven bee colonies, the same vibration energy of 18,000 Bovis units can be measured on the spot where they stand. The hives themselves show an energy of 180 million Bovis units. At the central stone where those energies come together the measured energy was even 1.8 billion Bovis units! The natural number 18 (2×9) as found in many plants and chemical structures is omnipresent here. Now the Bee-Sevenstar is obviously in a harmonic, natural balance.

Prospect

After a long conversation with the inventor of the Sevenstar, Mr. Heinrich Sannemann, on 21st June 2011, in his house in Bissendorf - he was already more than 90 years old at that time - gave his permission to pass on his knowledge because he wanted to help *Mother Earth* with many more Bee-Sevenstars. Now, the maximum active zone of a 13-metre Sevenstar is 9.2 km. It is possible to increase the diameter to 25m and have 13 instead of 7 bee colonies in it; that would create an active zone of 22km. To make that happen, the central stone has to go into the ground for 30cm and rise 70cm up into the air. With such a construction, it would be possible to harmonize an entire city.

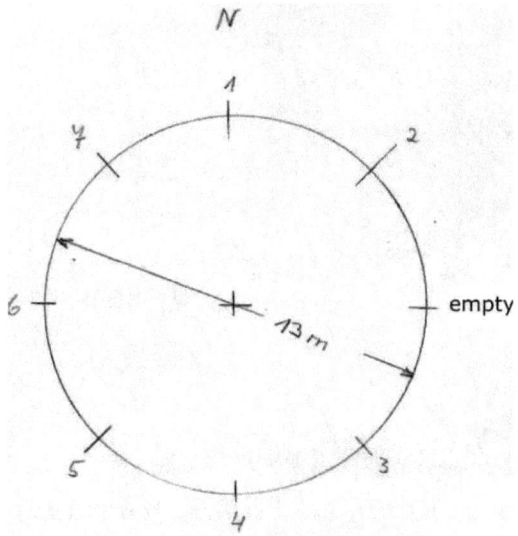

Another possibility which seems to be worth trying is to set up this asymmetric octogon with an empty space on its east side.

Bee-Sevenstar in Ratingen-Lintorf (Germany), 2010,
occupied by seven colonies in a circle of 13 metres diameter.
In the centre, the central stone is visible. I get the bees over
the winter by keeping them in two frames (German standard
size) and adding up to three more hive frames with middle
walls of wax during the year (including a grid for ant
protection). Those middle walls can be left out, but the
"honey harvest" would definitely become much more
difficult then.

What to do when you get a bee-sting?

A healing practitioner once told me about an ancient
"farmers' rule" (ancient farmers' knowledge often passed
down to next generations in poetry). An easy symbol from
our alphabet, painted on the sting spot, is already enough to
prevent the sting from swelling up. As you know, the stings
can swell up a lot otherwise, especially on the head or the

hands, i.e., anywhere where there is little muscle/fat cells and mostly skin.

This symbol looks approx. like the sinus sign or an inverted major "S" in the Latin alphabet ("Sig" rune in the old futhark). Just make it look approximately like in the sketching below. This will help immediately to prevent the swelling and it is free of any cost. Sounds unlikely?

I agree. Anyway, just try and see. If you are interested in symbol healing, read about the work of the Austrian electrician Erich Körbler. He did plenty of research on methods of information healing via symbols such as straight lines, "Y" shapes and "S" shapes and had many successful healings in practice backing his work.

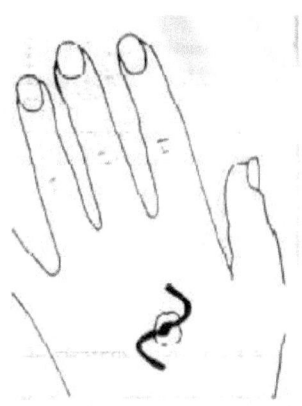

In the next sketch it is explained why this works. See how the cosmic energy is captured and amplified by some forms (like the "Sig" rune in this case).

→ cosmic energy

Ω Energy vortex

With this **S** *(sinus sign or Sig rune in the old nordic Futhark alphabet)*, the cosmic energies that come in from all sides can be *collected and concentrated*, as also happening inside a *wind or water vortex*. If you consider it more deeply, it is also not far away from the *infinity sign;* it just has been opened up.

13

Appendix

Excerpt from Maria Thun's book *Aussaattage* (sowing days):

The sidereal moon cycle

The moon passes the twelve regions of the zodiac in its 27-day long circle around the Earth, and while she does so, she imparts forces to the Earth that are expressed by the classical elements (fire, water, earth, air).

Those elements stimulate impulses in the four different organs of the plants (leaves, flowers, roots, fruits). By knowing about and taking into consideration those stimulants, we can support the plants' health in all acts of sowing, caretaking and harvesting.

Similarly, those forces affect the bee colonies. The bee colony closes itself to the outside and to energies from the outside by plugging the entire hive, except for the entrance, with *propolis*. Thus, if we open a hive frame for caretaking or harvesting jobs, a "chaos" will be created inside the hive (energetically speaking). Within this chaos a new cosmic impulse can be absorbed, and that impulse will be a guideline for the bees until the next time caretaking jobs are done.

Let's conclude the natural laws we have found through our experiments with plants and bees as well by observing weather phenomena in the following scheme:

Constellation	Element	Climate	Bees
Pisces	water	wet	honey care
Aries	warmth	warm	nectar collection
Taurus	earth	cool	comb building
Gemini	light	bright	pollen collection
Cancer	water	wet	honey care
Leo	warmth	warm	nectar collection
Virgo	earth	cool	comb building
Libra	light	bright	pollen collection
Scorpio	water	wet	honey care
Sagittarius	warmth	warm	nectar collection
Capricorn	earth	cool	comb building
Aquarius	light	bright	pollen collection

Frequencies

1.) Bred queen and her colony: 450 Hz
2.) Swarm queen and her colony: 642 Hz
3.) Sevenstar queen and her colony (while in intermediate time for active Sevenstar): 999.9 kHz
4.) Swarm colony in fully active Sevenstar: 1,321 kHz
5.) Earth's frequency: 850 Hz
6.) Varroa mite (6 Hz below animals' frequency → parasite!): 444 Hz
7.) Average honey: 900–1,700 Bovis units (B.U.)
8.) Sevenstar honey: 9,500–100,000 B.U.
9.) Sevenstar tip: 1,321 kHz / 210,000 B.U.
10.) Sevenstar centre: 999.9 kHz / 105,000 B.U.
11.) Sevenstar tip without bees: 6,200 B.U.
12.) Earth frequency near Sevenstar: 25,000 B.U.
13.) Sevenstar with iron ring around it: 995 million B.U.
14.) Sevenstar with double spiral antenna: 1.8 billion B.U.

14

Literature

Charpentier, Louis
Das Geheimnis der Kathedrale von Chartres
Knaur Taschenbuch

Lakhovsky, Georges
Das Geheimnis des Lebens
VGM Verlag, Essen

Neumann, Erich
Inspirationen aus der Vorzeit
EFODON e. V. 82383 Hohenpeissenberg
ISBN 3-932539-07-9

Neumann, Erich
Auf den Spuren der Feinkrafttechnik
zu beziehen bei
Hugo Grote, 59581 Warstein/Niederbergheim,
Oberbergheimerstr. 1

Risi, Armin
Machtwechsel auf der Erde
Gowinda Verlag

Sannemann, Heinrich
Der Bien und seine wahre Aufgabe auf Erden
Printed in *Heinrich Sannemann* Nr. 1, Verlag: tredition.de

Der Stern von Bethlehem
Heft 8 der gelben Reihe, 2004
Printed in *Heinrich Sannemann* Nr. 2, Verlag: tredition.de

Schintling-Horny, V. v.
Steinkreise helfen Mutter Erde
like a Stone Circle Stonehenge
and *Allkraft.* Five Stone Circle around a garden
Verlag: tredition.de, Hamburg

Seeley, Thomas
Honigbienen
Birkhauser Verlag, 1997

Simonis, Werner Christian
Erde, Mensch und Krankheit, 1974

Mellinger Verlag Stuttgart
Milch und Honig
Verlag Freies Geistesleben Stuttgart, 1965

Thun, Mathias K.
Die Biene, Haltung und Pflege
M. Thun Verlag 35205 Biedenkopf, 2000

A Sevenstar can be found at
Volker von Schintling-Horny
Hülsenbergweg 110
40885 Ratingen
Tel. 02102 37805 Fax 02102 37949
schintling@schintlinghorny.de

"Seven Star Foundation"
Treuhandstiftung BienenSiebenStern Zorneding
Gründer: Harald Habeder
Herzog-Otto-Weg 39
85604 Zorneding E-Mail: info@bienensiebenstern-stiftung.de
Tel. +49 (0)171 4518 555

Books by Volker von Schintling-Horny

Gespräch zwischen Vater und Sohn
3. Auflage 2004, LSH Verlag
Hier habe ich mit einem Sohn das fiktive Gespräch auf folgende Themen gerichtet:
ein Blick in die Zukunft, Kunst, Frankfurter Schule, Insider, Israel, Gelddruckerei, kommender Erlöser, Gruppendynamik, Mauerfall, Briefe an die Kinder

260 Seiten   € 26,00

Naturkundliches
2. Auflage 2004/2009, LSH Verlag
Zusammenfassung der Kräuter und Rutengänger Seminare von Irmgart und Hugo Grote in Föckinghausen, Sauerland, 1995 bis 2012, Auszüge aus Schriften von Heinrich Sannemann über Ernährung, Bäume, Wasser, Licht.

196 Seiten   € 22,90

Gute Gedanken aufgelesen
2. Auflage 2008/2010, LSH Verlag
Kunst, Politik, Familie, Benker Kuben, Weisheit.
Auszüge aus Seminaren und Schriften sowie viele
Tipps zu unseren täglichen Fragen

396 Seiten   € 29,90

Das Leben eines immerfort strebenden Lausbuben
1. Auflage 2010, LSH Verlag
Meine Lebenserinnerungen in Wort und Bild,
angefangen von der Kindheit über Schulzeit, Studium,
Beruf und Selbstständigkeit sowie Familie und Hobbys

376 Seiten   € 29,90

Schau ins Weltenwissen oder in die Akasha Chronik
1. Auflage 2010, LSH Verlag
Alles ästhetisch Vertretbare ist aus dem großen
Weltgedächtnis abrufbar mit Gefühl, Muskeltest, Rute,
Pendel, Traum, Rumpelstilzchen Tanz, Benker Kuben,
Schlafplatz.

83 Seiten   € 15,50

Lebensenergie
1. Auflage 2010, LSH Verlag
Leben mit Energie, Energiekreise, Symbolenergien von Runen, Bäume als Energieanzeiger, Benker Kuben, Huna-Energie der Polynesier

206 Seiten   € 22,90

Runen und andere Energiewandler
1. Auflage 2009, LSH Verlag
Futhark, Formenenergie, Bauernhäuser, Runengymnastik, Tonkrüge

84 Seiten   € 22,90

Lehren der Einweihung
1. Auflage 2018, LSH Verlag
Hier sind die Einweihungsriten der Essener, Indianer, Ägypter und vieler anderer in Auszügen der Originaltexte erzählt.

230 Seiten,   € 20,00

Obige Bücher sind zu bestellen bei:
Verfasser:
Volker von Schintling-Horny, Hülsenbergweg 110, 40885 Ratingen
E-Mail: schintling@schintlinghorny.de
Telefon: 02102 31110   Fax: 02102 34458

Die folgenden neun Bücher sind direkt im Verlag zu bestellen unter
www.tredition.de
E-Mail: info@tredition.de
Verlag: tredition GmbH, Halenreihe 42, 22359 Hamburg

Der Bien im Siebenstern
14. Auflage 2002/2014, tredition Verlag, Hamburg
Aufstellen der Honig-Bienenkästen im Siebenstern-Kreis harmonisiert Mutter Erde und hilft ihr, die täglich zugeführten Umweltschäden zu überleben.
ISBN 978-3-8495-7665-3 Paperback   € 15,00
100 Seiten

Musik ist Leben
1. Auflage 2015, tredition Verlag, Hamburg
Überall wo der göttliche goldene Schnitt mitklingt, ist Leben. Das Waldhorn, Sphärenklänge an unseres Daseins Grenzen, mathematische Strukturen, Harmonieweisheit, Notation.
ISBN 978-37323-2963-2 Paperback   € 12,95
      978-37323-2964-9 Hardcover,   € 17,75
      978-37323-2965-6 E-Books   € 2,99
146 Seiten

Gymnasium der Reife Ohne Arzt, ohne Pillen – aber in Harmonie und mit Gott – das Alter beenden.
1. Auflage 2016, tredition Verlag, Hamburg
Jedermann ab 50 Jahren braucht dieses Gymnasium für seine richtige Ernährung, Bewegung des Körpers und Geistes, der ewigen Seele, des vergänglichen Körpers, Geburt und Tod.
ISBN 978-37345-0144-9 Paperback   € 16,99
      978-37345-0145-6 Hardcover   € 24,99
180 Seiten

Steinkreise helfen Mutter Erde, die ihr ständig zugeführten Umweltschäden zu überleben.
2. Auflage 2017, tredition Verlag Hamburg
Steinkreise sind Energiebündler, Bovis Skala, Schaltstein, Boitiner Steinkreise. Externsteine, Pyramidendreieck, Energietransport. Leylinien.
ISBN 978-3-7439-7143-1 (Paperback) € 19,50
       978-3-7439-7144-8 (Hardcover) € 25,50
       978-3-7439-7145-5 (E-Book) € 3,99
108 Seiten

Heinrich Sannemann
Heiler, Weiser, Wissender, Imker, Naturforscher.
Band 1, 1. Auflage 2017, tredition Verlag, Hamburg
Schriften der Gelben Reihe Heft 1 bis 4.
Der Bien und seine wahre Aufgabe auf Erden, die Entwicklung des Planeten Erde, Vater, wir preisen Dich, Gott sprach: Lasst uns Menschen machen nach unserem Bilde.
ISBN 978-3-7439-5222-5 (Paperback) € 24,95
       978-3-7439-5223-2 (Hardcover) € 29,31
       978-3-7439-5224-9 (E-Book) € 2,99
740 Seiten

Heinrich Sannemann
Heiler, Weiser, Wissender, Imker, Naturforscher.
Band 2, 1 Auflage 2017, tredition Verlag, Hamburg
Schriften der Gelben Reihe Heft 5 bis 7.
Die Wiederbelebung unseres Erdbodens, Belehrungen für den Jetzt-Zeit-Menschen 1, Belehrungen für den Jetzt-Zeit-Menschen 2, Der Stern von Bethlehem leuchtet.
ISBN 978-3-7439-5769-5 (Paperback) € 24,99
       978-3-7439-5770-1 (Hardcover) € 29,99
       978-3-7439-5771-8 (E-Book) € 3,99
674 Seiten

Heinrich Sannemann

Heiler, Weiser, Wissender, Imker, Naturforscher.
Band 3, 1. Auflage 2017, tredition Verlag, Hamburg
Schriften der Blauen Reihe Heft 1 bis 3 und der
Grünen Reihe Heft 1.
Wachet auf, Sehnsucht nach Liebe, Auf dem Weg
zum Licht und Unsere Arbeit
ISBN   978-3-7439-6150-0 (Paperback) € 19,99
          978-3-7439-6151-7 (Hardcover) € 23,99
          978-3-7439-6152-4 (E-Book)   € 4,99
376 Seiten

Heinrich Sannemann

Heiler, Weiser, Wissender, Imker, Naturforscher
mit dem *Neuen Nachrichten* **Band 4,** 1. Auflage
2017, tredition Verlag, Hamburg
ISBN   978-3-7439- 7896-6 (Paperback)   € 19,00
          978-3-7439-7897-3 (Hardcover)   € 25,00
          978-3-7439-7898-0 (E-Book)   € 4,00
352 Seiten

Hier beschreibt Heinrich Sannemann unser Weltgeschehen in der
letzten Phase, **U-Boot und Flugscheiben-Antriebe,** Gesundheit und
sein Lieblingsthema Wasser. Damit sind nun alle Schriften von
Heinrich Sannemann in Band 1: Gelbe Reihe 1, Band 2: Gelbe Reihe 2,
Band 3: Blaue und Grüne Reihe und Band 4: Neue Nachrichten
zusammengefasst.

ALL-KRAFT

1. Auflage 2018, tredition Verlag, Hamburg
Kräfte und Energien aus dem All auf der Erde gebündelt und nutzbringend eingesetzt. Fünf Steinkreise erzeugen ein Land der Kraft für starke Nahrung.
www.tredition.de oder E-Mail: info@tredition.de
Dort im Shop oder unter www: schintlinghorny.de
Webseite: Literatur/Beiträge informative Leseprobe starten. Inhalt: Die Harmonisierung vom Gemüsegarten bis zu 80 ha großen Ackerflächen mit dem Erfolg, weniger Dünger und weniger Spritzmittel einsetzen zu müssen, oder bessere Heilungschancen in Krankenhäusern, besserer Notendurchschnitt in Schulen sowie die Magnetschwebebahn aus der Megalithzeit. Sehr lesenswert und zukunftsweisend.

ISBN 978-3-7469-7023-3 (Paperback)   € 19,99
        978-3-7469-7024-0 (Hardcover)   € 28,50
        978-3-7469-7025-7 (E-Book)   € 4,99
240 Seiten

Zeitfracht Medien GmbH
Ferdinand-Jühlke-Straße 7
99095 Erfurt, Deutschland
produktsicherheit@kolibri360.de